MISSIONS OF WAR

by Robert J. Brodersen

InfusedMedia Co. LLC
www.infusedmedia.co
1-888-251-6088

Missions of War: A Personal Journal of World War II Missions
Robert J. Brodersen
Fulfilled by: Sara Brodersen Cameron

"This book is one of a kind and it's filled with stellar first-hand description of events that happened during the World War II. It is the kind of book that you don't want to put down as it captures the depths of your soul. The military history was spectacular and readers are being kept in a wave of understandable level of enthusiasm through its tactical level of writing. Totally recommending this book to everyone, it's powerful and engaging!"

- Allison D. Steeley

"I can say, it's a story that's needed to be written in history books. It offers readers a new sense of perspective of what really happened during World War II. Readers will get a good dose of what it's like to be in a combative set-up during a war. The introspective, personal account in the storyline is such an eye-opener which is totally relevant to the current issues of today. I'm giving this book five-stars!"

- George Oliver A. Grahame

"Strongly recommending this book without reservations! It's a must for those military buffs and readers who are into combat aviation and military cultures. For me, I find this book to be truly persuasive and this memoir exposes the trials and tribulations a soldier has to face in the midst of a war. It's a gripping firsthand account from a soldier's family, and I admired the writing. The book's message is unflinching and so powerful, you should try reading it!"

- Seymour T. Edstrom Jr.

"The act of patriotism is highlighted in the story. If given the right audience, this book deserves to be made into a movie, surely, it's a blast! The author offers one of the most soaring definitions of what it means to SERVE YOUR COUNTRY. This is the story that we all need right now, it's life-changing and should remain as a constant reminder for us to always dream for greatness. This book will forever have a place in my heart."

- Charlemagne D. Ackerman

"Such an inspiring story about a man and his determination and persistence to realize his dreams and fight for the honor of his beloved country. The book is filled with great adventures and honestly, I was having a hard time putting it down. The incredible journey of a patriotic man should be shared to the whole world. Going to war is just the easy part, I've learned that coming home to your loved ones is the hardest part of all."

- Jake Sheldon R. Wilman

Introduction to Missions of War

In this second edition of Robert J. Brodersen's Diary of Missions, we, the children of Robert would like to include a bit of his life before and after the missions. We hope to share what led up to his stint in the Army and some of his personal life.

Robert James Brodersen was born May 27th, 1921 to James and Sadie (Cameron) Brodersen, the youngest of six children. The eldest was half-sister May Brodersen Van Valin, followed by 3 brothers, Riley, Charles, Malcolm, sister, Harriet Ruth (died from scarlet fever at age 3), and then Robert. All were born on the family farm, homesteaded by his Grandfather Rasmus Brodersen, 7 miles southwest of Herman, in east central Nebraska.

Bob attended Brodersen School through 8th grade, just up the road from home. Grandpa Rasmus had donated some land for the school, as many settlers did, hence its name. Bob always said the main disadvantage to living so close to school was that his family would provide the teacher room and board. This meant there were no school secrets kept from his parents, and trouble at school meant trouble at home! He attended grades 9 and 10 at New England Country School and graduated from Herman High School in 1938.

Bob was reportedly a bit mischievous as a boy and always enjoyed a good laugh. He talked many times about his favorite pony, which he often he rode to his best friend Sonny Rogert's house. One crisp morning, as he and Sonny drove his pony and cart to school, the cart upset when they took the New England corner too fast. Teacher Miss Elsie Wilson, rushed to see if they were all right. Bob stayed on the ground, according to Miss Wilson. He didn't want to get up.

She was afraid he was injured, but when he finally got up, was noted to be covering up spilled cigarettes. We're not sure what happened next, but Miss Wilson usually left an impression!

Bob worked for his Uncle Frank Brodersen summers and while going to high school. There were enough men to do the farm work in Bob's family, with his dad and 3 older brothers. Bob mentioned several times how nice Uncle Frank and Aunt Mary were, and they lived just a couple miles away from home. Everyone farmed with teams of horses, and the tractor age was just beginning.

In the fall of 1938, Bob headed off to Wayne State College, intending to become a teacher. Those plans changed when he and his roommate, Axon from Norfolk, were talking one day about the war heating up in Europe. They were pretty sure that the United States would get involved and reportedly looked at each other and said, "We need to be a part of this, let's enlist!"

Bob and Axon enlisted in the army and reported to Fort Crook, Omaha in the Spring of 1939. Bob always referred to him as Ax, and we can't recall his first name. They rode a troop train to Fort Lewis, Washington. It was there that Pvt. Brodersen trained, learning to be a radio operator. One day some officers came into class to ask if any of the boys would like to learn to fly. Bob said he thought for a minute and raised his hand. He said he figured why not, he was already further from home than he ever imagined. If they thought they could teach a Nebraska farm boy to fly, it might as well be him!

Following that, Bob and another buddy Bob Clark, asked their sergeant if they could report for the pilot sign-up, but he wouldn't allow it. They snuck out and butted their way into the office to sign up. They did get into a little trouble for bucking the chain of command, reportedly with some KP (peeling potatoes or dish duty). They found out the requirement for pilot training was 2 years of college, or take some courses to pass a test. Clark had the college, but Bob B. had to do the courses and test. After a bit they were in! (The Army Air Corps, part of the Army, was the forerunner of the Air Force.)

From there, they went to Fort Ord, California. Bob referred to it as a big "Tent City". Although we aren't sure of dates, they were then transferred to Cheyenne, Wyoming for more flight training. The last leg of training took place in Sioux City, Iowa, from which there are some familiar stories.

One such tale was when Bob was flying south of Sioux City one day, and he decided to buzz Herman. He flew over New England School and farm places along the way. Chickens scattered and livestock stampeded while the area folks looked up in amazement at the huge bird, the B-17 flying over so low. Some were scared it might be the enemy, but we have personal accounts that it was that "ornery Bobby Brodersen!" He did get a bit of a reprimand from that but said it was definitely worth it!

Just a sad note on Bob's friend, Axon. They were separated in training with Axon ending up in Texas. He was tragically killed in a training accident there. Bob did keep in contact with Axon's mother, and they shared a lot of memories and tears in later years. Bob Clark went on to become a flight instructor, training many of the pilots needed to keep the Army Air Corps supplied.

Robert Brodersen went on to pilot a B-17 over enemy-occupied Europe during the dark days of World War II. That is where his story starts now, as he so thoughtfully kept a diary of his missions. We hope you will enjoy and appreciate it as much as his family does. He would be proud to know we shared it with you.

Sara Brodersen Cameron

The crew: top row left to right, Brodersen, co-pilot; Meade, navigator; McCall, pilot; Hall, Bombardier; bottom row, Albert, waste gunner, Kinny, tail gunner; Whalen,turret gunner; Lon Quan, radioman and top gunner; Atchue, engineer and top gunner; Connally, gunner; and McDougall, waste gunner.

Missions of War

BY ROBERT J. BRODERSEN

In World War II, I served a tour of combat missions over occupied Europe. I kept a diary of the missions, which were written on some loose sheets of paper and very poorly organized for someone else to read. I am rewriting them with the thought that they might interest some of my descendants in the years to come. In rewriting them, I will fill in some of the human interest sidelights involving the crew which I hope you will find interesting. Keep in mind that it is now the winter of 1981-82, and these experiences were in the year of 1944.

The first week of January, 1944, our crew was sent to Kearney, Nebraska to fly a new B-17 bomber to England and be assigned to a bomber group for combat duty. We had just completed two months of training as a crew, and we were ready for action. Our crew consisted of ten men:

McCall (Mac)... Pilot
Brodersen (Brodie)................................... Co-pilot

Meade (Fuz)..	Navigator (nose gunner)
Fryer...	Bombardier (nose gunner)
Atchue...	Engineer (top turret gunner)
Whalen..	Bottom turret gunner
Albert...	Waste gunner
Kinney..	Tail gunner
Lee (Lon Quan)...	Radioman and top gunner
McDougall..	Waste gunner

We were somewhat nervous concerning the trip to England because we were routed over what they called the northern route, and this being the dead of winter made it somewhat dangerous. The safer route would have been south over the southern route through a much warmer climate, making our chances of survival much better in case we crashed in the ocean. Replacements were badly needed, and the northern route was shorter and, of course, quicker.

Our first leg was from Kearney to the state of Vermont, and it was beautiful. Snowfall had been heavy, and the pine trees were loaded with it, making it a beautiful scene...like the ones you see on a Christmas card.

Our next leg was from Vermont to Presque Isle, Maine, and not quite as pretty but getting colder and tension was starting to build as our next leg was to take us to Goose Bay, Labrador. Our flight was mostly over Greenland which is nothing but mountains covered with snow. They warned us to be sure the plane was in tip-top shape because the area we were flying over was unpopulated, and if we went down they would be unable to rescue us and temperatures were down to 40° below zero.

The trip was successful, but Goose Bay was a small Eskimo village and the United States had built a runway and put up a few buildings. It was a very rugged outpost. After we parked the plane, a truck came out to pick us up to take us to the barracks, and the truck driver was an Eskimo. It would have been better if he had some dogs and a sled, but he did manage to herd us over to the barracks; I don't know what language he spoke, but it sure wasn't English.

We spent several days at Goose Bay preparing for the final leg of our trip to England. We flew this entire trip alone, not in sight of any of our planes, so our flight planning had to be exact. We took off in the morning darkness because the days were very short this time of year in the far north. As it grew light, we could see the vast North Atlantic Ocean below us with huge icebergs floating everywhere, just one big "Tom Collins" on the rocks, I guess.

We were flying at 12,000 feet and after several hours a cloud layer formed below us so we couldn't see the ocean . . . really kind of a relief. Then in front of us a red distress flare came up through the clouds. This is fired from a hand gun which is standard equipment for every airplane to carry. This meant, of course, that an airplane was down in the ocean and was pleading for help. It would be similar to the roman candles we had for the Fourth of July celebrations, only many times more powerful.

We were told at our briefing at Goose Bay to ignore this because it could be a surfaced German sub trying to lure us down below the clouds and then they would try to shoot us down. We followed instructions and stayed straight on our course, but in our minds it was very distressing not to know but that it could very well have been a plane like ours . . . down in the North Atlantic with survival chances of zero. We couldn't have helped them. We were never able to find out if this was a decoy by the Germans or a genuine distress.

Our navigator, "Fuz," was quite nervous, because if we were off just merely a degree on our heading, we would miss England and end up in Nazi-held Europe. The war would have been over for us, so we really put the pressure on him. After many hours of flying, and as we approached within about 500 miles of England, we were able to pick up a radio signal beamed from England which we could follow to bring us in. The only hitch was the Germans could do the same thing and lead us right on by England. Our heading was correct and it brought us right in on the nose. But the airport that we were supposed to use was covered with bad weather. In fact, all of England was weathered in, and we were instructed to proceed to the New Hebrides Islands which were off the extreme northern tip of the English Isles.

Airplanes preparing to land.

We stayed on top of the weather as we headed north, and after several hours we decided to let down through the clouds. When we finally broke through, we were flying down a valley with very high hills on each side reaching up into the clouds. This was pure luck, a one in a hundred lucky break.

We landed at a R.A.F. base (English Air Force) and had our first sample of tea and English chow. It was very different than back home, but we ate it like we liked it.

In several days the weather cleared, and we took off for England proper and delivered our plane to the 8th Air Force. We then rode a train to Northern Ireland, to a base to be assigned to a Bomber Group. We stayed there several days being processed, and, while there, we were approached by some Irish civilians wanting to know if we would like to attend their church on Sunday. I don't remember the denomination of the church, and I really didn't care because I thought basically they all had the right idea. We all thought it was a good idea, after our close call over the New Hebrides, and we should give our Maker some credit.

We were all settled in the church and the preacher started the sermon, doing real well, and all of a sudden, an Irishman right behind us jumped up and said "Praise the Special Name". We all rose up out of the pew like we had been shot. We got settled back for a few minutes and another jumped up and said "Amen". This kept up during the sermon and we sat there waiting for the next blast. I don't mean to be making fun of those people, but we weren't accustomed to this. It did have its good point though . . . nobody went to sleep.

From Northern Ireland, we were sent to Horham, Suffolk, England to the 95th Bomb Group, 336 Bomb Squadron. This was about 100 miles north of London in the middle of farming country. Small farms, about 60 acres each, dotted the countryside with narrow roads winding around and through small rolling hills. It was really quite pretty.

Located about every 3 miles or so would be a pub (beer joint). Their beer came in large barrels which they served at room temperature. If we would have a cold spell they would light several candles under the beer to keep it from getting cold. Every pub had a dart board on the wall complete with darts, and everyone was welcome to play. It soon developed into a gambling game, the loser buying the beer.

The English liked their beer, and in the evening there would be farmers, the local blacksmith, storekeeper and, of course, some American Air Force men. Needless to say, the English bought very little beer, because they were really good at darts. They would bring their set of darts which they carried in their pocket in a small case.

Their beer was rationed out to the pubs and would last about four days, so they would be out for the rest of the week. If it hadn't been for the Yanks, they wouldn't be out, and this did upset the local people.

We were assigned sleeping quarters, and Mac and I roomed together. All shades were tightly closed at night so that absolutely no light showed to the outside. The reason for this was the German Air Force was very active at night and they might spot the light and bring about a raid on the air base. All forms of light were forbidden, even flash lights. The headlights on all forms of transportation were blacked out, so it was quite an experience.

In a few days we were all checked in, and an airplane was assigned to us. This base being a bomber base, it had all Boeing B-17's, the same plane that we trained in and flew over to England in. It was called a heavy bomber, four engines and carried a crew of ten. It was armed with ten 50-calibre machine guns, carried around three ton of bombs and about 1,500 gallons of gasoline. It cruised at about 180-mph and would climb to about 30,000 feet. At that time it was one of the best airplanes the U.S had.

Everything was set now, and our crew was put on the list for combat duty. They told us if we could make it through 25 combat missions we would be sent back to the States. We visited with some of the crews that had already flown some missions, and that left us somewhat demoralized. Losses had been heavy. The German fighter planes were very rough and the anti-aircraft fire was severe over the target areas. The German anti-aircraft guns could fire shells up as high as we could fly and then they would explode, scattering shrapnel (small pieces of jagged metal) all over the sky.

They had bulletin boards in each barracks area, and we were to check this each evening to see if we were scheduled to fly the next morning and what time to get up. They would wake us up about three hours before take-off, so if take-off time was at 5 a.m. we would be awakened at 2 a.m. This involved having breakfast, then briefing us on our target, how many enemy aircraft we could expect, number of enemy anti-aircraft guns around the target and back, altitude, weather, the amount and size of our bomb load, the number of our planes involved, where in the formation we would fly and on and on. It would take us about 2 hours to climb to 25,000 feet and we had to be that high when we hit the coastline.

We were issued escape packets before each mission. This was like a heavy envelope that would fit in your pocket, and each man received one. In this envelope was money, the kind used in each country over which we might fly.

These envelopes were sealed, and you were not to open them unless you were shot down. This money was to be used to buy help for you to escape. The escape route was through France and over the mountains into Spain, which was neutral, and then the Spanish would return you to England. Quite a trick I would say, but not impossible, some did make it. As you know, Germany occupied all of Western Europe except Spain and Switzerland. We were briefed by several men that made it and they were real hair raisers. They told us if we were shot down and bailed out to delay opening our parachute until very low. You were to judge this by watching the trees and buildings, and when they were easy to see in detail, then pull the rip cord. When we hit the ground we were to gather up our chute and hide in bushes, trees, buildings, culverts, just anywhere and be very quiet. The reason for delaying opening the chute was so you spent the least time possible in the air; therefore, if there wasn't a German patrol very close, you had some time to hide.

When darkness fell, there would be a very good chance that someone would contact you from the underground movement. This could be France, Belgium, Denmark, Holland, Netherlands or any other German occupied country. They would instruct you as to what to do, which was usually walking at night toward Spain. In your escape packet was a compass, map, and some chocolate bars. The money was most important when you came to the border of Spain, as it was very mountainous and dangerous, and you had to have a

Lt. Brodersen at ease.

guide. There was an airman from Herman, Nebr. by the name of McConnaha who made it all the way to the mountainous Spanish border, but then fell from a high mountain trail and was killed.

If you bailed out over Germany, it was a different story. If you spotted a military installation while floating down in your parachute, you were to head for it and give yourself up. The reason for this was that many civilians had been hurt and killed by our bombs, and the population was very unfriendly. Some of our boys had encountered groups of farmers with pitchforks or worse yet, groups of young boys in the 12-14 year old bracket, and it was quite possible they might harm or kill you unless rescued by the German military. With all this information under our belt, some of our patriotism may have lessened, but we were anxious to get started, and that we did.

Mission Number 1

TARGET - BERLIN

On the evening of March 9, 1944, I checked the flight board for the next day and my name was on it. Not the crew, but just me. I was listed as "tail gunner". I was certainly confused, but the next morning straightened it all out. Our commander was to lead the raid on Berlin and he wanted a pilot for a tail gunner, thinking a pilot would be better qualified to tell him how the formations behind us were doing. The tail gunner has two 50-calibre guns in his position and a large man wouldn't fit in the tail gun position.

I was awakened at 5 a.m. and went to the mess hall to eat breakfast. The mess hall was for men on combat duty that day, and we had fried eggs, any way you wanted them. This was a luxury enjoyed only by the combat crews, and I hadn't eaten anything but powdered eggs since leaving the States. This was the breakfast served before every combat mission, but only to the men that were flying. This was really more important to the morale than you might think. For a few minutes, it took your mind off of the uncertain future that day.

Upon finishing breakfast, we went to the briefing room and you are not told your target for the day until this time. When all the men were in the room, seated and the doors closed, the briefing officer pulls the curtains back, disclosing a map of Europe and lines running from England to Berlin. This brought forth loud moans from the men because Berlin was a tough target. Back in the States, the people were led to believe the men stood and cheered when informed they were going to bomb Berlin, but this was not so.

I met the Commander, and he told me what he wanted from me. He is not able to see to the rear, and he wanted me to be his eyes. He would want to know how the planes behind were doing, and he wanted them flying a very close formation. He wanted to know if any of our planes were shot down, enemy fighters and if it looked like they were going to attack my formation.

A "squadron" was made up of six bombers. A "group" was made up of three squadrons totaling 18 planes. A "wing" consisted of three groups totaling 54. We were the lead plane of this wing. This wing flew in a very tight formation for defensive power.

Behind us several miles was another wing and several miles behind that was another and behind were more, how many I do not know. It was not unusual to send three to five hundred bombers to a target the size of Berlin.

So, sitting in the lead plane, this twenty-three year old Nebraska farm boy had some view. In my wildest dreams, never did I think of seeing a thing like this. Only four years ago I was working for my Uncle Frank Brodersen on a hill farm in Nebraska for thirty dollars a month. I had only been out of Nebraska twice in my life and that was to follow the harvest north to Minnesota with my best friend Sonny Rogert, and the other time was to just cross the Blair Bridge into Iowa. These things did cross my mind, and it was difficult to add them up to this situation.

I am going to copy word for word the notes I made after our return from the raid.

"Take off 8:00 a.m. position "tail gunner". Losses: eight bombers. Considering the deep penetration, it was an easy mission. No fighters were encountered, but the flak was quite nasty. Three bursts came close enough to hear. What a sound-sort of chills your insides-sounds like the woof of a big dog. And the tinkle of pieces of metal could be heard against the airplane. I amused myself by shaking my fists at nasty flak puffs and cursed it under my breath. I defied the stuff to come any closer; what a laugh. It was really a milk run, no holes in the plane-only twenty four more to go. "I hope."

Robert J. Brodersen

The losses of eight bombers that I mentioned in my notes were planes from the wings that were behind us. They had a very rough mission. A plane smoking and in flames going down from twenty-five thousand feet can be seen from many miles away, and gives one a very sick feeling because you know all the boys didn't have a chance to bail out. Our target was the railway yards which were located in the center of Berlin. So you can see, if we missed the target proper, they would surely hit somewhere in the city limits. We usually dropped our bombs so that they were strung out when they hit the ground.

Eight hours and fifteen minutes after take-off, we landed back at our base. Trucks met us at our planes and took us to what was called a de-briefing room. There was an "Intelligence Officer" assigned to debrief each crew. We were each served a shot of whiskey to relax us, and then he wanted to know everything we saw.

B-17-E Boeing Flying Fortress - World's Deadliest Bomber

How many enemy aircraft, accuracy and intensity of the anti-aircraft guns, how many planes we saw go down, both friendly and enemy and on and on. The above procedure was repeated after every mission.

"Copied from diary"

Raid Number 2

Wednesday, March 15, 1944

Target - Brunswick, Germany

Take-off   0700   Landed   1500   Total   8 hours

Position   Co-pilot   Losses   23 bombers

We were awakened at 3 a.m. and in our minds we thought "Berlin, here we come." I might add that this wasn't a happy thought. Only one thing nice about a mission, and that's the fried eggs for breakfast.

The raid was quite easy as far as we were concerned. Mac saw a U.S. P-38 nail a German F.W. 190 to the cross.

B-17s and bullets flying.

The raid was uneventful except for the above. The planes lost were not from our group.

Raid Number 3

Thursday, March 16, 1944

Target - Augsburg, Germany

Take-off   0700   Landed   1630   Total   9 hours 30 minutes

Position   Co-pilot   Losses   23 bombers

This was indeed a deep penetration, clear to the southern part of Germany. We really had a horseshoe in our pocket. We didn't fly with our own group but were attached to another. We could see large formations of B-17s on both sides, and our escort looked beautiful. Then we looked around a few minutes later and they were gone. I guess we hadn't flown for five minutes when the enemy fighters began to hit us. No attacks were made directly against our group, but the groups around were really catching hell.

We are missing six B-17s from our group including our squadron commander. Some of the planes in the 95th group were in bad shape. We were damn lucky to be flying with another outfit. Our crew got out without a scratch.

I saw some German rocket ships (ME 2100) firing at a group below us and some ME 110s blasting hell out of a poor straggler—the last I saw of him he was going straight down and not because he wanted to. The guy that said the Luftwaffe is beaten is a damn liar.

I find out now that we have to do 30 missions now instead of 25, which leaves me 27 to go.

Raid Number 4

Saturday, March 18, 1944

Target - Munich, Germany

Take-off   1000   Landed   1845   Total   8 hours 45 minutes

Position   Co-pilot   Losses   43 bombers

This was another of those trips deep into the heart of Germany. We thought it might be cancelled due to bad weather, but no such luck. These long hauls are really trying on a guy. You sweat, your back aches, ears hurt and your eyes look like a couple of blood spots. What a way to earn a dollar.

Something happened to our fighter escort as we had none for two hours while in Germany. The Germans had their fighters and rocket ships up and gave some of the boys a bad time. We had two attacks against our squadron, one of them while I wasn't flying so I saw the whole show. Three German ME 109s came in on us head-on and things looked real sad. McCall threw the ship up and down in taking evasive action, and I guess that's the reason they didn't shoot us down.

Part of a group of B-17s.

The windshield in front of me shattered, but the bullet did not knock the window out. I checked my body over, just knowing I had been hit, but no blood. A window down in the navigator's compartment was also shattered, but no fatalities. The bomber flying on our left wing went down.

Atchue, our upper turret gunner, received credit for shooting one down and Whalen, our lower turret gunner, also received credit for one. Kinney, our tail gunner, got credit for a probable. Lee, our radio-gunner shot the aerial off of our own airplane, and he took a lot of kidding over that. His full name is Hon Quan Lee, and he lived in China until he was 12 years old. When getting excited he would mix some Chinese in with his English and it was a riot.

This kind of a mission makes a believer out of a guy. The flak over the target wasn't bad - only 26 more to go.

Shortly before going overseas, I was home for several days, and my mother gave me a pocket sized Bible which had a metal back on it. When preparing for a mission I always carried it in my left shirt pocket over my heart. This was a very special part of preparing myself for a mission, and it grew on me more and more as I progressed to the next mission.

My religious background was quite meager. My mother was very instrumental in organizing a Sunday school in our local eight grade country public school house (Brodersen School). I went there every Sunday morning until I left home at age fourteen. This I feel was the link that made this little Bible very special.

Raid Number 5

Sunday, March 19, 1944

Target - "Right across the channel"

Take-off   1500   Landed   1845   Total   3 hours 45 minutes

Losses   1 bomber

This was indeed a milk run, and we were happy to get it. The flak was accurate, but moderate. We received some battle damage––two holes in the wing from flak. The target was German submarine bases on the coastline. Only 25 more to go.

Raid Number 6

Sunday, March 23, 1944

Target - Brunswick, Germany

Take-off   0700   Landed   1345   Total   6 hours 45 minutes

Losses   27 bombers

This morning we dragged our tired fannies from the sack at 0200, what a heart breaker, as we were supposed to get a pass. This was a fairly short mission, but it was well into the German fighter belt. We felt better when considering our fighter escort.

Our group didn't receive any direct attacks from fighters but groups both ahead and behind us did. Our crew saw 13 bombers go down––very demoralizing.

We had two holes from flak, but they were quite small. One was beside the engineer's head in his top turret. Didn't hurt him, but he is indeed a believer. Only 24 to go.

We were notified that we had been given a three-day pass, so London, here we come! London is one large city, and we had heard some great stories from crews who had spent a three-day pass there.

We saw "Big Ben", a famous old clock and the changing of the guard at Buckingham palace and many bombed out buildings, which were the result of German bombing raids. London was still taking a beating from nighttime bombing raids, so we found out when we were to be on the receiving end.

The night life was great. In the center of London was an area called Piccadilly Square. It was full of nightspots, and they, in turn, were full of English girls. Yanks and service men from many countries of the world were there. Most of the service men were on three-day passes, so they were out for one big time. There was wine, women, song and a few fights thrown in.

Two of the fellows lined up a couple of girls' for the night for seven pounds, that being about thirty dollars. They went to the girls apartments and were just nicely settled in for the night when the air raid sirens started to blow. Everything was dark in the room and the girls jumped out of the bed and the fellows couldn't figure out right away where they went. They finally realized that the girls were under the bed, which would give you a certain amount of protection if a bomb fell nearby. So they jumped out of bed and crawled under, too. But by this time the girls were back in bed, cause the all clear siren was blowing. They claimed this happened three times during the night.

One night we were out on the streets, and the air raid sirens started to blow. We ran for the nearest subway station, as these were underground and made a good shelter. There were thousands of English civilians there and most of them asleep. Every night many of these people came here bringing a bed roll with them and spent the night.

Some of these people had been doing this for years. I didn't realize until then how much these people had suffered. In the morning they would go home and to their jobs. The Germans did very little bombing in the daytime because the loss of planes was too heavy.

We really enjoyed our pass, but it was over all too quickly and we hopped the train for the trip back to base and more missions. On March 26, the crew was awarded the "Air Medal" for completing 5 missions.

Raid Number 7

March 27, 1944

Target - Bordeaux, France

Take-off   0930   Landed   1900   Total   9 hours 30 minutes

Losses   1 bomber

This was a long haul, but it was a very easy mission. We hit an airfield, and I mean we obliterated the damn place. The weather was beautiful and France looked very beautiful and quiet. Only 23 to go.

I meant to mention this before. We lost our bombardier, Charles Fryer. He was flying with another crew that day . . . it was a raid on Berlin. No one knows what happened. He was a hell of a swell guy and the efficiency of our crew proves it. We have an enlisted gunner in his place now by the name of Elmer Connally.

Raid Number 8
April 1, 1944

Target - Brunswick, Germany

Take-off   0625   Landed   1035   Total   4 hours 10 minutes

I'm not sure this was mission no. 8. We failed to reach our objective due to bad weather. On March 26, the crew was awarded the "Air Medal" for completing five separate bomber combat missions. I think it would have been an easy mission, as the fighter support looked good, and I think we would have had an under cast, therefore keeping many of the German fighters on the ground.

We didn't drop our bombs as we were over occupied country. We saw some flak, none coming very close, so we may get credit.

We were awakened at 0145. Who was it that said "every day in the Army is like Sunday on the farm?"

Recall

Easter Sunday, April 9, 1944

Target – Poland

Take-off   0850   Landed   1145   Total   3 hours

"Old Bauldy," our beautiful silver ship, made her last landing today. We started out on a long mission this morning (12 hrs). All went well until about 200 miles out over the North Sea and there we ran into some bad weather. The leader gave us orders to abandon the mission, drop our bombs in the North Sea and return to base.

We had a most unwelcome surprise upon reaching the coast of England. Our most dreaded enemy of all, "weather," was paying a visit. Visibility was about 1,000 feet and the ceiling about 200. We came very close to having several mid-air collisions before spotting a field. We came in over the runway and damned if there wasn't a B-24 bomber stopped right in the middle of it. We circled and tried another and this one had a building about half way down the runway. This left one more runway to try and it was quite short, which we soon found out. We landed about 1/3 of the way down, but when we applied the brakes, she didn't slow like it should have because the runways were slick. This air base was under construction and there was a ditch about 10 feet deep at the end of the runway. We hit the end of the runway going about 50-mph and it was too much for "Old Bauldy". Her nose dug into the soft mud and her tail went up to nearly a vertical position before settling back.

Fire broke out immediately between no. 1 and 2 engines. It was indeed a mad rush in leaving "Old Bauldy," and it was certainly a relief to see that everyone was accounted for. The only injury was sustained by the bombardier, Elmer Connally. Fuz and I carried him away from the plane as he couldn't walk, and we were expecting her to blow any minute. The hospital reports that one leg was fractured.

It was a sad sight watching her burn. There was about one thousand gallons of gas, thousands of rounds of 50 caliber bullets going off and many distress flares of all different colors going off. My final comment in my diary was, "All that's left of our big bird is a tail wheel——the rest of her is ashes. She was a good ship."

We now have 10 missions under our belt, we've lost two bombardiers. The first, Charles Freyer, was killed in action and now the second, Elmer Connally, injured in a plane crash. We will have another bombardier assigned to our crew and we will be given another plane.

Raid Number 11

Thursday, April 13, 1944

Target - Augsberg, South Germany

Take-off 1020 Landed 1800 Losses   plenty 33 bombers

We were awakened this morning at 0600. We were all very happy because we were all very positive that it would be a short raid.

It was indeed a low blow when the briefing officer told us that the target for today was Augsburg, south Germany, deep in the German fighter belt. This incidentally was our third trip to Augsburg, and this target is always good for some excitement.

We believe these are flak bursts from shots to the plane.

Our escort was really beautiful and for that we can be thankful. We saw about 10 German ME logs, but there were no direct attacks on us. The flak over the target was terrific. We had 3 holes in our plane, but they were quite small. We did pick some off the floor, enough for each of the crew to have several pieces. You see, it had enough power to come through the side of the airplane, but not enough to go through the other side.

McCall and I aged plenty on this mission, as both number 2 and 3 engines smoked badly and the superchargers had about a 6-inch surge. The flak had done some damage to the engines but not fatal. We fell back from the formation but not too far, and we were barely able to keep up. We were afraid we might become a straggler, meaning we would not be able to keep up, and then German fighters would all attack us like a bunch of vultures. A straggler would never make it back home from this distance.

One thing that proved very consoling on this trip was the fact Switzerland was only 10 minutes from our target. We could see

Lake Constance, a very large lake which separates Switzerland from Germany.

We did manage to stay reasonably close to our formation and made it back. We lost one airplane from our squadron, a new crew. I might add, if we had decided we couldn't make it back, we could try to make it to Switzerland. Switzerland was neutral, and if we had gone there we would have been interned for the rest of the war. Quite a temptation.

Raid Number 12

Tuesday, April 18, 1944

Target – Berlin

Take-off   0945   Landed   1800   Total   8 hours 15 minutes

We went to the big "B" today. The thought of big "B" makes the best of crews shudder, for she is known for her flak and fighter protection.

We were awakened at 0600 this morning. The morning was far too beautiful to risk one's own neck over Berlin, but what was there to do about it. It was beautiful weather all the way into the target. The fighter protection was fair, but the prop-wash from the wing ahead gave us a bad time. That is certainly mean stuff and exceedingly dangerous if you hit it in close formation.

At the target there was a huge cumulus cloud which made bombing impossible, so we bombed some smaller towns nearby. I can imagine how the Germans must hate us for that. I hope we missed as I doubt if there was anything of military importance there.

We were right at the target when enemy fighters were spotted. The crew saw about 50, all single engine jobs. That was indeed a tense moment. Attacks were made on the groups ahead and behind us, but I guess we had the old horseshoe along as our group received no attacks. I'm afraid the 8th Air Force lost plenty of aircraft, but our group came out okay . . . . Only 18 to go.

Raid Number 13
Wednesday, April 19, 1944

Target - Airfield just east of the Ruhr Valley (werl)

Take-off   0625   Landed   1300   Total   6 hours 35 minutes

An easy mission today, good for the morale after the trip to big "B" yesterday. This raid took us into the German fighter belt, but our escort was beautiful. No enemy aircraft was seen and very little flak.

The weather was swell and the only gripe is that we flew part of the way in that infernal prop wash. Oh yes, my "butt" hurts me. Big fires were left raging at the target. Only 17 more to go.

Raid Number 14

Thursday, April 20, 1944

Target - Cherbourg Peninsula, France

Take-off   1545   Landed   2045

This raid is classified as a "no-ball". Very short and easy. The type B-26s usually make. Our target consisted of rocket emplacements on the Cherbourg Peninsula, which is quite close to England. The raid was uneventful, very little flak. The only thing causing us to worry was the gas supply. We had about 15 minutes of gas left when we landed.

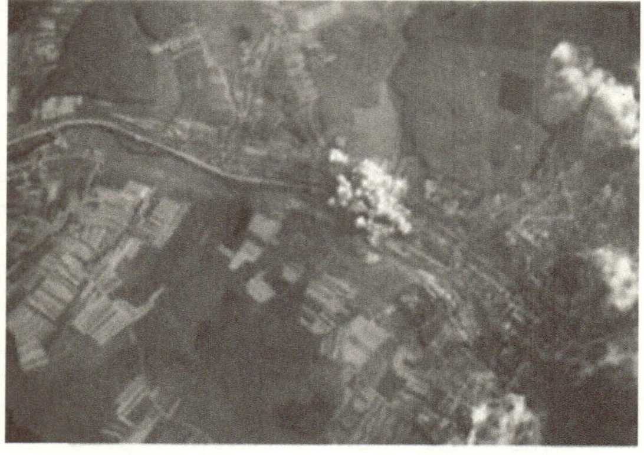

View from the plane, bombs bursting below. Bombed German railroad.

We carried a 1,000 lb. bomb under each wing and the three tons in the bomb bay. Only 16 more to go.

Raid Number 15

Saturday, April 22, 1944

Target - Ham, Germany Ruhr Valley

Take-off   1515   Landed   2200   Total   6 hours 45 minutes

We learned at the briefing this afternoon that our target was going to be the marshalling yards in the city of Ham. We all thought in our own minds that this really isn't such a bad mission, except that the flak might be a bit nasty. As for enemy fighters, well, we probably won't see any. We were certainly in for a surprise.

Today was a good day for flying and was a nice trip all the way to the target. Our group became confused at the target. Consequently, we did not hit it, but another group behind us did. We were about 5 minutes off the target when, down out of the sun, came about 30 enemy fighters, making a head-on attack on our group. Out of the corner of my eye I could see them coming. They looked to number in the hundreds to me. I was flying at the time. When our gunners began to fire, I took some mild evasive action, although I couldn't see what good it could possibly do. I was expecting the airplane to do anything but stay in one piece. Why we weren't fatally hit is beyond my power of reasoning. Maybe it's because we spend an hour in church every Sunday possible. The window directly in front of my position was badly shattered, a hole in the bombardier's section and six other holes in various parts of the ship. The only injury was sustained by the navigator, a slight cut above the eye. Two ships were shot down to our left and nearly every ship in the formation sustained battle damage of some degree. I'm certainly happy to mark off raid no. 15. Only 15 to go.

Raid Number 16
Monday, April 24, 1944

Target - Friedrichshafen, Germany

Take-off   0815   Landed   1710   Total   8 hours 55 minutes

It is apparent for the present at least, that "old man weather" is on our side. It was a beautiful day for flying, both to the target and return. Our target, Friedrichshafen, is (or was) located on the edge of Lake Constance, which forms the boundary between Switzerland and Germany.

Upon learning the whereabouts of our target this morning at briefing, I believe every man had a sick feeling in his guts, as it is a long way from England and smack in the fighter belt. The one and only consoling fact being, it's only 10 miles from the target to Switzerland.

We were crossing the border from France into south Germany when the fighters hit us. About 10 came in from 10 o'clock low. The bombardier and navigator got in a few nice bursts. They didn't see any fighters go down, and neither did we receive any damage.

The flak at the target was fairly accurate, but it was visible from the flak bursts that the Germans were confused by our chaff. On every mission, just a few miles from the target and while on our actual bombing run through the target, the waste gunners would throw out chaff. This was a metallic-like paper, and it would mess up the radar aiming device on the German anti-aircraft guns. This procedure was followed on all our missions.

We did receive one hit under no. 3 engine. It made a hell of a noise, and we thought it might be serious, but it only messed up our hydraulic system. The trip back was uneventful, as our escort was beautiful.

The coffee, doughnuts, and smiles from the Red Cross girls and a shot of scotch hit the spot, as we were a bunch of tired boys. Only 14 to go.

On May 2, 1944, our crew received another decoration. It was an Oak Leaf Cluster to the Air Medal which we were awarded on March 26.

We were also told that we would get to go to the "flak shack" for a week. This "flak shack" was a resort area on the west coast of England, and after completing about half of their missions, every crew got to spend a few days there. Its purpose was to pick up your morale and to settle down your nerves.

I had a big decision to make, and it was a very difficult one. I knew my brother Chuck was somewhere in southern England, along with about a million other Americans, waiting for D-day. My C.O. gave me permission to go if I wanted to, instead of going to the "flak shack," but he didn't think I would be able to find him. Everything was so secretive that no American servicemen were allowed to tell anyone his outfit,

Chuck and Bob Brodersen home on leave in Herman NE.

where they were located or any information, for fear that he might be a German spy. It was a court marshall offense.

I hopped on a train for southern England, and all I knew was that he was in a "tank destroyer" outfit. When I got to southern England I started asking questions, but none of the Yanks would tell me anything. So I dropped into a pub to have a beer, and it was full of Yanks. I could tell by their emblems if they were with a tank outfit, and these are the boys I zeroed in on. I sat down at their table and insisted on buying nearly every round and soon had made some friends. I finally got one of them to confide in me, and he told me where he thought Chuck might be and where I could catch a ride on a truck to that general area. It was more luck than sense because the truck took me right to his outfit. I checked at the "orderly room" and his C.O. sent a man to find him. I stood back out of sight when I saw him coming, and when he was very close, I stepped out in front of him. It was a very happy reunion. With only about half of my missions completed and "D-Day" coming up for Chuck, life was very uncertain for the both of us. I stayed several days and then had to head back to my base, but I know this did me more good than the "flak shack."

Raid Number 17

Monday, May 8, 1944

Target – Berlin

Take-off   0530   Landed   1440   Total   9 hours 10 minutes

Losses   36 bombers

This is the target that makes you stand up and say "Uncle".

The briefing went off okay this morning, nice fighter support and local weather, "Cavu" (clear). The plane checked out swell on the ground—everything set, which was quite in contrast to what happened yesterday. Our crew had our first abortion yesterday, spoiling our beautiful record. Our waste gunner had the bends yesterday and our oxygen system was faulty in the top turret.

Today was another day and all went well. We had a solid undercast after crossing the Belgium-German border so we bombed big "B" on radar. The boys spotted several large formations of enemy fighters, but none attacked our group. Our fighter support was beautiful. We led the high squadron today so Meade and I should be promoted 1st Lt. soon. Several groups had hell shot out of them, but as for us-we've still got the old horseshoe. No damage to our ship. Only 13 more to go.

Raid Number 18
Target - Liege, Belgium

Take-off   1440   Landed   2030   Total   5 hours 30 minutes

Losses   10 bombers

This was indeed a fine mission for our group, short, weather was fine. Fighter escort was beautiful. Our target was the marshalling yards, and they say we creamed the target. I saw a bomber in the lead group take a direct hit from flak beside the no. 1 engine. The wing came off and went into a spin. Our crew watched him spin to the ground and explode and no parachutes were noted.

Raid Number 19
May 12, 1944

Target – Czechoslovakia

Take-off   0845   Landed   1745   Total   9 hours 40 minutes

Position   Co-pilot   Losses   42 bombers   Altitude   23,000 feet

This was my first trip to Czechoslovakia and I hope my last. It's just too goddamn far from home. Six hundred-fifty airplane miles, to be exact. The weather was "cavu' (which means clear), and we hit our target - a synthetic oil plant and supposedly the largest in the world. Smoke from the target rose nearly to our altitude (23,000 ft). There is no question as to whether we demolished it or not. Jerry put on a big show for us today with his rocket guns. When they explode they look like an airplane enveloped in flames, tumbling end over end. Fifteen fighters hit us on our homeward trip. A very poor attack––like a group of green pilots. We are missing one plane from our squadron.

Our crew was awarded our 2nd Oak Leaf Cluster to the Air Medal on June 7, 1944.

We had payday today and were informed that we wouldn't have to fly for several days. We have a new bombardier by the name of Hall and he wanted me to go up to the club house and try our luck in a poker game. I never considered myself a good poker player, and he was even poorer. He insisted, so I thought, "What the heck".

We got into a high stakes game. The currency was, of course, English, and their smallest paper money was the pound, which was worth about four American dollars. The bad part of it is you start throwing those pounds around like they were dollars. We both were really lucky and were winning more than our share of pots. After several hours, I was ahead and I knew Hall was, too, so I told the other players that Hall and I had an appointment and we would try to return. Hall was about half sore at me for this, but on the way back to the barracks we counted up our winnings and he had made 500 dollars and I was 250 to the good. So needless to say, we were on cloud nine.

As we walked down the road the next morning, we could see an Englishman coming towards us driving a fine looking horse on a nice carriage. Hall says, "Let's buy that outfit." We hailed him down and told him what we wanted. He said, "I'm sorry lads, but this horse and buggy is not for sale, but I do have one back at the farm that I will part with." We made an appointment with him for the next morning.

Each crew was given two bicycles to use, so we lined up the bikes the next morning and went to see the man. He showed us a much older horse and buggy and I was disappointed. Hall was from the city and the only horse he had ever seen was from a distance. I checked her teeth and they were smooth so I knew she had seen better days. I told Hall her teeth were smooth, but that didn't mean a thing to him, he thought she had pretty teeth. The Englishman wanted 65 pounds, which figured out to about 250 dollars. I didn't have any luck jewing him down, cause Hall wouldn't keep his money in his pocket. We bought the outfit and proceeded to harness her up and hitch her to a two-wheeled cart. It was a real riot as Hall didn't know the horse collar from a bridle. The horse didn't have any shoes on her, and the roads were all hard-surfaced, so this was a must. The Englishman directed us to the nearest blacksmith shop. We tied the bikes over the back and off we went, leaving a smiling and very happy Englishman.

As we were traveling to the blacksmith shop, we were deciding on a name for our new horse. It was a mare so we settled for the name of "Queenie". She trotted along at a nice gait and it was a scenic ride. The roads were narrow, hard-surfaced roads that continually wound back and forth through small rolling hills. This was farming country and small farms dotted the hills on every side. The blacksmith was a very curious fellow. He wanted to know who we bought her from, how much we paid, where we were going to keep her, and on and on. We told him everything except the price. We knew we had paid too much, but we were happy, so we thought we had a bargain.

We received a big reception upon arriving at the base. The guys yelled and clapped and laughed. Winston Churchill wouldn't have received a more vocal reception. Of course, there were some off-colored remarks, but we figured those guys were just jealous.

We found a long rope and tied "Queenie" behind the barracks as there was grass everywhere. Every day that we didn't have to fly we would harness her up and go for a ride to town or to the local pub, which was about two miles up the road. She was a very gentle horse and quite smart, too. When coming

Hall and Brodie with Queenie

home from the pub after dark, she would take all the correct turns back to the barracks without any help from the driver. Whether at home or away, someone was always petting her and she loved it.

Raid Number 20

May 25, 1944

Take-off   0420   Landed   1050   Total   6 hours 30 minutes

Losses   0   Altitude   24,000 feet

Raid number 20 was certainly a difficult mission to complete. This morning being the fifth time that we have gotten up at one a.m., only to have it scrubbed at take-off time. This morning we made it. The seemingly almost impossible twentieth, and it proved to be an easy one––short with no flak and no enemy fighters.

Our target was the marshalling yards at Brussels. The weather was beautiful, just a few scattered clouds at 10,000 feet. The bombs from our group fell short of their mark, but the other two groups hit the yards okay. Only 10 more to go.

Raid Number 21

May 30, 1944

Target - Brussels, Belgium

Take-off   0700   Landed   1145   Total   4 hours 45 minutes

Losses   0

We have been exceedingly fortunate in having two easy missions in a row. We went back to hit the marshalling yards at Brussels. We missed the last time. The weather was swell, meager flak and no enemy fighters. Nine more to go.

Raid Number 22
June 4, 1944

Take-off   0915   Landed   1430   Total   5 hours 15 minutes

Position   Co-pilot

This was a no ball, our target being pillboxes and flak batteries on the Belgium coast. There is a reason for the welcome short missions and that being the nasty flak. Our altitude of 25,000 feet kills their accuracy, consequently it's not too hazardous.

We had to make two runs on the target, due to broken clouds at 10,000 feet, and this always invites trouble. "Herman" really had our speed and altitude on the second run. We didn't suffer any losses, but several of our planes received some nasty hits. We ran head-on into a group of B-24 bombers, often referred to as "geese", on our return. Brother, that ain't good. We didn't collide, but it wasn't our fault. Our flak-happy bombardier (Domanick), nearly went wild, as he has only one more mission to go. We have eight more to go.

Raid Number 23
D-Day, June 6, 1944

Take-off   0330   Landed   1040   Total   7 hours 10 minutes

Altitude   16,000 feet

Every crew, despite their dislike towards a mission, wouldn't have missed this one for the world.

D-day, invasion day, the day that seemingly would never arrive, is now a reality. When our target was disclosed at briefing, everyone stood and cheered, despite the hour of 0100. When one thinks of the thousands of guys hitting the coast this morning, it makes one realize he is not alone. Those boys are giving their all for Uncle Sam.

Our target was the estuary of the River Orne. We were all terribly disappointed, as there was an undercast over the beachhead making it impossible to witness the invasion fleet. We dropped our bombs, (4 tons) on radar and good results were reported. It had to be good as we were bombing some 800 yards ahead of our assault barges. We encountered no flak or fighters. I wonder if Brother Chuck is down there with his tanks? I wish he was flying with me now. It would be safer.

We were told nearly every bomber and fighter in England would be flying today. Our route was laid out for us and we were told to follow it. If we had engine trouble or any other problem, we were not to turn around and come back. If we did turn around, we would be shot down.

McCall is beginning to have trouble with his nerves. He is taking medication at bedtime so that he can sleep. It is becoming difficult for him to fly the airplane. Our last mission we took off at 0330 a.m. It was very dark, with very few lights and with a full bomb load. This is a pressure situation. He took the plane down the runway, lifted off and then screamed for me to take the controls. We were probably forty feet off the ground and I didn't know how much pressure he had on the controls, making it an extremely dangerous situation. The plane dropped slightly, but I was able to recover before hitting the ground.

McCall is an honest man and he was doing his best, but the pressure of all our missions was getting him down. We were very close friends and we talked about his condition. He agreed that I should make all take-offs and landings and he would fly as much as he could. I loved to fly the airplane, but on long missions, which were always flown in formation, it was almost more than I could physically endure. After a long mission my eyes would be black, just like I had been in a fight. The short missions I could handle. We hoped his medication would help and take it one mission at a time.

The crew was awarded a 3rd Oak Leaf Cluster to the Air Medal. This is pretty much an automatic award given as you continued to complete your missions.

Raid Number 24
Thursday, June 8, 1944

Take-off   0500   Landed   1200   Total   7 hours

Our target today was a railroad yard at Tours which was about 70 miles behind our lines. The channel was clear today, making it possible to get a good view of the invasion coast. A guy really doesn't see much though––thousands of boats of all sizes. If it hadn't been that the boys across the channel needed us, we would never have taken off this morning (nobody is risking). The clouds were solid from the ground up to 24,500 feet. There were hundreds of bombers climbing to this altitude and it was dark so you could not see one another. Another bomber came so close to us that we heard the roar of its engines but never did see it. It had to be that it passed just a few feet above us.

We broke through at 24,500 feet and then were able to get into formation. The lead plane would fire certain colored flares so we would know which plane to get into formation with. It was a very nerve-racking experience to say the least.

From the channel and across France the clouds were broken and the target was clear. We really creamed the railroad junction, our load being one ton bombs. Flak was meager, no fighters, just a milk run. Six more to go.

Raid Number 25

June 12, 1944

Target - Airfield in France

Take-off   0430   Landed   1800   Total   8 hours

Position   Co-pilot   Losses   33 bombers

The Luftwaffe is supposedly moving closer to the coast in an effort to support the German ground troops against our beachhead. The weather was lousy, which prevented us from hitting our primary target. We dropped our bombs on an airfield which was clear. Flak was negligible and no enemy fighters were seen.

Our group received several days rest which meant no flying, so the USO, or some similar organization, lined up a big party involving a dance with a big name band. Girls from all over this part of England were brought by bus and rail. The dance turned out to be a special thing for me.

A dance like this was somewhat one-sided as the fellows would outnumber the girls, about three or four to one. The girls were instructed by the organizers that they were to dance with any fellow who asked, and not to team up with one guy.

The Air Force had quite a few fellows who considered themselves Romeos, had a line of baloney, did seem to have a way with some women, and usually were successful. I am not really a shy fellow, but I just didn't try that hard, and, more often than not, I didn't end up with a girl.

The girls and fellows were mingling on the dance floor before the dance started, and I spotted a girl who looked like Betty Davis, the movie star. I got up all my courage and asked her for the first dance, and she readily accepted. After we completed the set, I bought her a drink, visited a bit and then the band struck up again. One of my Romeo friends asked her to dance and she accepted.

I stayed by the bar visiting with some of my friends, happy that I had danced with this beautiful girl and decided the competition was too great to dance any more. When this dance set was over, low and behold, here she came back to me and really was friendly, completely ignoring my Romeo friend. We danced again, and between dances she attracted a lot of attention. She told them she was my girl. Needless to say, I was on Cloud Nine. She always came back to me between dances and danced with me every third dance.

After the dance, she had to ride the train some ninety miles back home. I didn't try to stay in contact with her because my tour of missions were about over, and I was afraid of a war time romance. She was the nicest person that I met in England.

Raid Number 26
June 14, 1944

Target - Airfield at Liege

Take-off   0330   Landed   0945   Total   6 hours 15 minutes

We were the lead plane in the tight squadron. The weather was again troublesome today. We had to climb from our scheduled 23,000 feet to 27,000 to clear the high, billowing clouds. We were fortunate——the target was fairly clear, with clouds on either side.

The mission was a milk run——meager inaccurate flak. Except for a near mid-air collision, the trip was uneventful. Four more to go . . . . . . maybe.

We have been driving Queenie three or four times a week, and she started to thin down a little too much. She was getting so she would much sooner walk than run. The grass was getting rather short around the barracks. The farmers raised mostly small grain, and they were cutting it with a binder. We would make a mental note of a field on the way to a pub in the evening, and on the way home after dark we would stop and throw on a few bundles. These were nice, heavy oats bundles and they did Queenie a lot of good. Wasn't long before she was trotting again.

We received some very sad news. All combat crews would now have to fly 35 combat missions before going back to the states. This is really very demoralizing, because originally 25 missions were considered a tour. Then it was raised to 30, and now 35. They undoubtedly have very good reasons for doing this, but eventually one's luck may run out.

Raid Number 27

June 15, 1944

Target - Hanover, Germany

Take-off   0340   Landed   1225   Total   8 hours 45 minutes

Seemed a bit odd to see the old tape stretch out across Germany after having shorter missions in support of "D-day". Plenty of ships have gone down in hitting this target or other targets of approximately the same geographical location. This wasn't our exact reason for being uneasy. The Luftwaffe has had a rest since D-day and we wondered.

The weather was swell for flying. We made a night take-off and assembled at 12,000 feet at daybreak. It is really a nightmare climbing in the dark with hundreds of aircraft going in every direction, not to mention those damnable intruders. For the last three mornings we've seen ships blow up, maybe from a collision or possibly an intruder. One can't tell in the dark.

We had an undercast on the entire trip this morning, preventing us from hitting the oil refinery, so we bombed the city on instruments. We didn't see any enemy fighters and flak was meager, but other groups weren't quite so fortunate. I see by the papers that the 8th Air Force lost 43 bombers.

Raid Number 28

June 20, 1944

Target - Oberslafen, Germany

Take-off   0410   Landed   1230   Total   8 hours 20 minutes

Altitude   24,000 feet

This target was (is or was) in the same locality as the last (North Germany). The weather was swell—not a cloud in the target area. We creamed our target with one-ton bombs.

The 8th Air Force certainly had a field day in North Germany. We saw two large factories burning on our return. We had been bombing ball bearing plants. If we can run them short of ball bearings, it will slow up their war machine.

We saw a few F.W. 190s near the target area, but they had their hands full, as some of our P-51s were keeping company with them.

Flak was moderate and we received no battle damage. McCall, the pilot has been getting worse; we talked it over and he agreed to go see the flight surgeon. I told him I would back him up because his nerves are shot, and he is not only dangerous to himself but also the crew. He was sent to a hospital in England, and through the use of drugs and tests they determined for sure that he wasn't faking it. This is standing procedure, because some will try it, and this way they supposedly know for sure.

I was assigned the position of pilot and a new co-pilot was assigned to the crew. The first mission with him was a complete failure. As we climbed to altitude he told me he was having the bends and could not stand the pain. I called the squadron leader and told him we were aborting and this really upset him. I was called into his office the next morning and after explaining the situation, he told me, "You should have taken him along because he had done this before". I told the squadron commander that I hoped to never see that man again. We were then assigned another co-pilot and he turned out to be just great. He had been a flying staff sergeant and was now a warrant officer.

Raid Number 29
July 14, 1944

Total   9 hours 15 minutes   Position   pilot

My first raid serving in the capacity of pilot. Crew undoubtedly questioned my ability, but believe they were well satisfied as all went off okay.

The crew was awarded a 4th Oak Leaf Cluster to the Air Medal. We are running out of room for the clusters on the medal.

Raid Number 30

July 18, 1944

Target - South of Parts, 40 miles

Take-off   0630   Landed   1345   Total   7 hours 15 minutes

This was a comparatively easy raid. Our target was a bridge which we missed because of a malfunction in the lead ship. Our ship was equipped with a camera, permitting us to return early. Weather was lousy, visibility being about one mile and ceiling 500 feet, making it very difficult to find the field. We experienced two near mid-air collisions with B-24s, but finally got her home all in one piece. We have 5 more raids to go.

Our crew has reached a milestone for which we are very proud. We were awarded the "Distinguished Flying Cross". This decoration did not come lightly as we have completed 30 missions under very dangerous conditions. Part of this can be contributed to luck, but much has to be credited to one of the finest crews in the Air Force. I was most fortunate to have such a crew like this, and I feel each man owes his life to the rest of the crew.

Raid Number 31

Target - Beachhead

The purpose of this raid was for support of the ground troops in Normandy. A very important one, also very easy, short and not too hazardous. Like so many of our missions, old man weather held the winning hand. We had an almost solid undercast, making it impossible to drop the bombs. We returned with the bombs, maybe this day wasn't meant for killing. We were to drop our bombs directly ahead of our troops but could not on account of the clouds.

It did count as a mission so now have four more to go. We will never be able to finish if they keep raising the number of missions.

Our horse Queenie is again losing weight. The English farmers thrashed their oats so she hasn't been getting any oat bundles anymore. While eating breakfast with Hall this morning we were discussing what we could find Queenie to eat as grass wasn't enough to keep her in shape. For breakfast at the mess hall there was always a big box of corn flakes on the table and got the idea Queenie might just like them. We took a box back to barracks for her, and she just loved them. We tore the top of the box open and we couldn't get her head out till she ate them all. We brought her a box every morning, and in a few days she started to get her strength back. It was a miracle.

Our base has been given several days of rest so another big dance was to be held. Hall thought we should try to line up a couple of girls that lived in a small town a few miles away and take them home with Queenie and our cart. We agreed that if we could line up two girls that he would take the taller one and I the shorter, which made good sense. He being taller than I and also eliminating any arguments over which girl each was to have. We hadn't been to the dance an hour and here came Hall looking for me, all excited, and he said he had us all fixed up.

He hurried me across the floor to meet the girls. One was taller than the other so there was no argument there, but the taller one was about 35-40 years old and the shorter one looked about 16. It worried me a bit about how old my girl was, but they all assured me that there was no problem. I was 23 and Hall about the same age as I.

We danced until about midnight, and the girls were good dancers and very friendly. We had a good time. So we all got in the cart and headed for their town which was about 5 miles distance. I want to remind you, there were no outside lights in England––boy, was it dark. But Queenie was sure-footed. Hall was driving, and when out in the country several miles he stopped to park, hoping to engage in some love-making. His girl insisted that she had to go home, and my girl was very bashful at this point, so things weren't working out too well. We weren't about to give up and gave them some arguments. After a time they told us why they had to go home. Would you believe we had a mother and her daughter for dates? After the shock was over, we all got to laughing about the situation and took them on home. They were nice people and insisted we come over to see them on a day off and they would fix a picnic dinner and tour the countryside with old Queenie and the cart. We intend to keep this date.

Raid Number 32
Target - Mersburg, Germany

Take-off   0445   Landed   1345   Total   9 hours

Our target for today was an oil refinery, one which we've been after for some time, but always in vain. I'm afraid it was the same story again today as we had a solid undercast.

In all 32 missions, this one was the most uncomfortable one. I've never before seen such wicked, accurate flak. When the stuff exploded, it was accompanied by a huge sheet of flame which threw our B-17 around like a kite. I thought this kid was going to knock on those pearly gates. I wasn't exactly scared as I was too busy keeping our plane right side up. But I was extremely uncomfortable. We had numerous holes in the plane, but luckily, none were fatal. We picked up numerous pieces of jagged metal off the floor of the plane which were pieces of German shells. Time for the sack.

Raid Number 33
Target - Munich, Germany

Take-off   0835   Landed   1735   Total   9 hours

Altitude   25,000 feet

What a heartache to find this target waiting us this morning at briefing. Now that it's over, I am glad, though. As I look back now, it wasn't so bad, but the potential danger was indeed tiring. Fighters, flak and a long way from home and who in the hell gives a damn. Tomorrow someone will pick up the paper and say, "Oh well, who cares." We bombed through the undercast, but guess we hit the city okay as the blind bombing equipment is fairly accurate and Munich is big. It was a very lonely, weird feeling— flying between cloud banks which towered to some 30,000 feet and hear the flak pepper against the airplane. We had several holes. Two more missions and back to the hills of Nebraska. I shaved this afternoon before going to bed, which I don't usually do because one is completely exhausted after a 9-hour mission. It really worried me what I saw in the mirror. My eyes were completely black. I looked like a broken man and it scared me. After a bit, I got hold of myself and made up my mind I had the stuff it took to hang on, and I wouldn't let my crew down. This is the closest I ever came to breaking down.

I thought of McCall and what he went through when he felt he couldn't go on. I've never held this against him for one moment. It was more difficult for him than it was for me as he was engaged to a wonderful girl by the name of Helen Urbanus, who we got acquainted with while training in Sioux City, Iowa, and they were going to be married when he came home.

I really got an insight into this as I was assigned to censor mail that the boys wrote home. The reason for censoring the mail was to cut out any reference to the war from which the enemy might benefit. Of course, I didn't censor any mail that McCall or anyone else that I knew wrote. I would have flatly refused. I could hardly believe how lovesick and heartbroken some of the boys were.

Brodie as a new officer.

I didn't have this problem. My mother and I corresponded, and she kept me informed how the crops were doing, the hogs, cattle and the general health of the community, which I did enjoy hearing about. I did hear from a neighbor girl occasionally by the name of Tootie Rogert, the sister of my best friend, Sonny. Their land bordered ours and we grew up together, she being about two years younger. From her, I found out how and what my generation was doing. She was a very fine young lady, and her letters really boosted my morale. I shall never forget her for this.

The squadron commander called me into his office and told me that there was a shuttle raid to Russia coming up and it would involve 4 raids. We would drop bombs on the way to Russia, land in Russia, load up again and bomb the Eastern front, go back to Russia, load up again and bomb another target and land in Italy. There we would load up again and bomb on our way to England. I already had 33 missions in, so this would make me 37, two more than I had to do. He told me I could rightfully refuse and there would be no hard feelings.

I talked it over with the crew, and most of the boys had 31 missions, I had gained one mission when I rode tail gunner to Berlin and gained another one because they had missed a mission on account of sickness. They told me they would like to go, and this would complete everyone's mission except for Hall, the bombardier, and our co-pilot, (I can't remember his name) as they were replacements on crew. There were still 8 original crew members. We had been through it all together and they were afraid bad luck would befall us if we broke up when I quit at 35. It was a tough decision, but I knew if I didn't go and we were split up and then they were shot down, I would never forget, so Russia here we come.

Hall and I had to make arrangements for Queenie's care while we were gone. She had eaten about all the grass around the barracks and we were getting a lot of complaints about the flies and gnats from all the horse manure. There was a farmer who lived about 20 rods from our barracks so I went over to see if he would pasture Queenie for so much a week until we returned. Boy, was he hard to visit with. The English out in the farm country had a terrific accent and used a lot of slang. I made a deal with him so we didn't have to worry about her.

Raid Number 34

August 6, 1944

Target - Rahmex, Poland

Total   10 hours 35 minutes

We were briefed this morning for a shuttle raid to Russia, and everyone was quite enthused over it. We were given P-51 escort and they did a beautiful job as we only saw 2 enemy planes. Flak was moderate and the target was thoroughly hit. After we crossed over the eastern front into Russia, we encountered some flak. It wasn't real close, and we wondered if the Russians were welcoming us or if they were that lousy of shots. This part of Russia had been occupied at one time by the Germans and now they had been drawn back. As we passed over cities and towns, it looked as if they were rebuilding, but that wasn't the case. All the floors had been blown out of the buildings, just leaving the walls standing. The destruction was terrible.

We found our airport at Poltava, Russia and this was some experience. They had rolled out steel matting, but didn't bother to level out the high spots. I no more than got the plane on the ground, and we hit a high spot, and we were airborne again. It's a good thing the B-17 is a good solid plane.

This evening a Russian soldier came around and asked if anyone would like to go to town and have a drink. There wasn't anything else to do, so he loaded our crew into a truck and away we went. They had set up a bar, a few tables, and chairs in a bombed out building and several Russians were playing in a small band. They brought us a round of drinks and, boy, were they strong. We managed to drink them, and here came another round. Several, which include myself, refused to drink the third round, but not Hall. He thought they were good and he thought the Russians would be intimidated if we didn't drink it all gone. So, he took it upon himself to finish the drinks for everyone who didn't want any more. It was now time to meet the truck, and we were walking to the street corner. We took a head count and Hall wasn't with us. We looked back down the street and there he stood. Said he couldn't move. Before we got back to him he started backing up, faster and faster until he fell on his back. He had passed out, so we carried him to the truck and threw him in. He will never live this down.

Raid Number 35

August 7, 1944

Target - Trizebina, Germany

Total   9 hours 35 minutes

We were briefed this morning in an old bombed Russian theatre. It was beautiful weather for bombing, and we creamed an airport in Germany. This evening, the Russians put on a show for us at the Air Base. They seemed to be grand people. They have a wonderful sense of humor, seem like Americans. They danced and sang Russian songs with lots of gusto. The women are really built stout, large busts and hips of which they are quite proud. When they smiled they had several teeth missing, making them look plenty tough. They are a rugged and very reckless people. They lost so many friends and family that they do very foolish things. One

Brodie relaxing after a grueling mission.

of the things they did made us shudder. They hauled the bombs out to load in our plane in an old truck. The driver would pull up by our airplane and a helper would just roll the bombs out back of the truck, letting them fall a good three feet onto the hard ground. The bombs weren't fused, but you just don't handle them like that.

Raid Number 36

Thursday, August 8, 1944

Target - Buzair, Rumania

Total   10 hours

This morning we took off for Foggia, Italy. On the way we bombed Buzair,

A few of the crew with the Russian women during
the shuttle raid to Russia.

Rumania, and tonight we land in Italy. We bombed an airfield on the way with very good results. Flak was moderate, and we sustained a weak fighter attack. Tomorrow we are going swimming in the Adriatic. We deserve a day of rest.

Foggia, Italy was located on the lower part of Italy. The climate was warm, with lots of sunshine. We were here four days and went swimming in the sea, also drank some Italian wine.

Raid Number 37
August 12, 1944

Target - Toulouse, France

Our target today is an airfield in German occupied France, and we will land back in England. This will be the final mission of our tour for 8 members of the crew. When we reached the English Channel we opened a bottle of beer we had brought from Italy. We forgot how the beer would act at 12,000 feet. It went wild with foam. We passed it from one to another while holding our hand over the opening. Needless to say more beer hit the walls and ceiling than anyone's mouth, but nobody cared. We sang songs as we let down and prepared to make our last landing

Brodie on a base bicycle, main mode of transportation before Queenie.

in England. We talked about how we would enjoy our meal at the "Lucky Bastards Table". As our wheels touched the runway, I'm sure my eyes were wet because I just finished a part of my life I shall never forget. Tonight we shall celebrate.

Robert J. Brodersen

Post Missions

Following the last mission, the crew was happily able to depart for home. According to crew member, Paul Albert's journal, "Tour of Duty" they packed up for a train ride to Glasgow, Scotland to board the Queen Mary for a cruise to New York. Paul states "There was an eight day delay which we never understood. Eventually we crossed the Atlantic to Halifax, Nova Scotia, where we learned of the delay; Winston Churchill was aboard for one of his famous conferences with President Roosevelt. Imagine! Making us wait a week for Churchill."

Albert continues, "After a joyful whistle blowing ride past the Statue of Liberty into the New York harbor, we were disembarked quickly and taken to camp Kilmer, New Jersey... we were furloughed for 15 days at home."

We are not sure how or when Bob got to go home on leave, but do know he was stationed in Florida for the remainder of the war. It was there he was able to catch up with his old buddy Bob Clark, who was a flight instructor during much of the war.

An additional note, before being assigned to a crew and sent to England, in March of 1942 1sst Lt Brodersen reportedly flew reconnaissance missions off the coast of Florida, training with the

Doolittle group. Bob wasn't in the final selection for the Doolittle Raid to Japan, but he did say it was frightening to see burning ships which had been hit by German Subs off the coast of Florida. It made him wonder if we would actually win the war.

But win we did, and on May 8, 1945, the war was officially over in Europe.

Bob was on his way home in July 1945 when he learned that his father had died. State Patrols were on the lookout for him to give him the sad news. He did arrive home in time for the funeral. It was a difficult time, but he was thankful to be safely home, as was his brother Chuck, who had been in a tank division in the war in Europe.

Bob operated the Herman Appliance store for Kenneth Punk Freeman upon his return home. He enjoyed delivering appliances and furniture to area customers. He got his furniture from the old Beebee and Runyon Warehouse in Omaha. Bob was somewhat a local hero, as were many of the returning veterans. He reportedly wore his leather flight jacket which impressed certain admirers.

One such admirer was a young Pearl Lang. She was a 1944 grad of Herman High and was currently working for her parents, Ernest and Emma on the farm south of Herman. Bob and Pearl began a courtship which led to marriage May 23, 1948 at Trinity Lutheran Church in Blair. They resided in the apartment above the old Post Office in Herman until an opportunity to farm came up later that year.

Bob and Pearl moved to a farm just west of Tekamah, which is now the Northridge Golf Course. Bob went to the GI farming school taught in Tekamah, to give returning vets an opportunity to brush up on the latest farming practices.

The Brodersens resided on that farm for 4 years, during which time 3 children were born. Joan, Mike, and Sara rounded out the family, and moved closer to Herman in 1953. Bob farmed with his brothers Riley, Chuck, and Malcolm, sharing equipment and labor.

The 1950s were somewhat lean years on the farm. Bob received notice in1951 from the Army Air Corps he was needed during the Korean War. He was able to opt out, with his farming and young family, although he did briefly consider going back in. Bob never did fly a plane again, even though a couple of Air Corps veterans, who had a grass air strip up the road, invited him to fly. Apparently, he closed that chapter in his life, never really saying why, except he was busy farming.

In 1962 Bob and Pearl achieved a life-long dream of purchasing a farm, west of Tekamah. They raised hogs, cattle, sheep, and chickens. They were very successful, winning awards in soil conservation, and other achievements. Bob was one who liked hiring folks down on their luck, in hopes of giving them a break, as well as his receiving some needed help. They would share our meals, and sometimes stay at our house.

One such employee was Joe. He was of a darker skin, like from India or such, and wasn't much taller than us kids. He was very soft hearted, and when we kids cried if a critter died, Joe cried along with us. Just as he could cry, he could have the most contagious giggle, which would make even the most serious person laugh. We remember a time when the polio vaccine was first distributed, at the Tekamah City auditorium in the early '60s. It was intended to be for locals, and our family was there with Grandma Sadie Brodersen, and Joe. As we stood in line, Bob told the registration folks that Joe was one of brother Riley's boys! We laughed about that for years. There are lots of Joe stories, but that could be another book!

Pearl was always good hearted about Bob's employees. She really knew how to stretch the dishes, so that whoever happened to stop by at meal time was welcome. There's nothing like the kitchen table to bring out the best in a group. Bob and his brothers hashed out many farming plans and politics, all the while rolling Prince Albert cigarettes, drinking coffee, and doing some occasional cussing. We kids experienced a lot of life and relationships around that kitchen table. Sadly, after 44 years of marriage and a short battle with cancer, Pearl died on January 17, 1993.

Bob and Pearl on their 40th Anniversary

Thirty Eighth Mission

Bob always wanted to see what Europe looked like on the ground, and in early 1996 enthusiastically signed up for the Heartland of Europe tour with the Washington County Bank in Blair, calling it his 38th Mission. Daughter Sara got to be his co-pilot. By the date of the tour, Bob began having difficulty with his balance and some memory loss. They took his diary along, and everyone on the Washington County Bank of Blair tour group read it. They seemed to appreciate the book and his accomplishments.

Bob did seem to enjoy most of that trip, and we could compare the locations of his missions to where we were on our tour. We traveled on a tour bus from Amsterdam, Netherlands, to Zurich, Switzerland, to Venice, Italy, to Vienna, Austria, and to Prague in the Czech Republic, touring and staying at different hotels. We were kept pretty busy. Bob made the comment one morning, "You know if we go to bed much later and get up much earlier, it's not going to pay to go to bed."

We continued to Nuremberg, Germany to Munich, and back to Zurich to catch a train traveling through Germany at night. In the morning we took a ferry to Copenhagen, Denmark. Our Brodersen family originally came from Denmark in the Schleswig Holstein area, so it was interesting to note the similarities of the area to Nebraska with the farming and livestock.

Bob and Sara in Europe

It was a wonderful trip, whenever someone asked Bob about it, he would just say, "You'll have to ask Sara." In the Czech Republic, when we were on this confusing road of several overpasses nearing Prague, I commented I was sure glad we were on the bus and not driving. Bob replied, "Yah, we would probably be fighting by now." And we both laughed.

In April of 1997, Bob suffered a fall with a back injury and entered a nursing home for recuperation. Due to balance and memory problems, he has resided there since. He was a resident at Oakland Heights, where he would enjoy a joke and had that twinkle in his eyes on the good days. He continued to live like he always did, one day at a time, up until his death, December 21, 2008, just one day after our family gathered for Christmas with him.

Robert has left a great legacy, in addition to his 3 children, there were 12 grandchildren, 15 great grands, and 8 great-great grands. We think about the terrible danger of being on a B-17 crew, where the odds of being shot down were great, and of all others fighting in wars. We are so grateful our father survived his time in the service and also for sharing his story. Simply amazing.

We would like to give special thanks to Chris Christen Nelson and Kurt Keeler and Crew from Omaha for all their hard work, to produce and perform "Missions of War, Above and Beyond", at the Nebraska State Fair, and in Tekamah for Veterans Day 2005. (Chris took on that project after reading Bob's

Diary when her father Hans Christen, and Bob were roommates at the Oakland Heights.) You have truly gone above and beyond what is asked of you and we thank you.

Brodie and Kurt Keeler playing the part of Brodie 2005

Chris Christen, producer of the Veterans Day Missions program
with Bob and Kurt Keeler,
who played the part of Brodie.

Bob with children, Joan, Mike and Sara at the Veterans Day
Program

The Reunion

Albert, Brodie and Kinney 1996 reunion

Just prior to our "38th Mission" to Europe, Bob hosted a small reunion with 2 members of his original crew, Daniel Kinney and Paul Albert. Albert had been corresponding with Dan Kinney and located Brodie via the internet. Albert had contacted Bob's nephew, also Robert Brodersen, at O'Neill, NE, asking if he was a B-17 pilot in WWII. He said "No, but I know where he is!"

Albert and Kinney arrived in Omaha in May 1996, where Bob and Sara picked them up. The three veterans had not seen each other in 55 years, when the war was over. They were the only members of the crew who could be located, but they still had a wonderful reunion. We kids and our families were included. It was amazing to hear the stories! As Kinney said, "It's as if we had never lost touch."

After Albert and Kinney's visit and receiving a copy of the Brodie's book, each wrote their memories down from their enlistment and time with the crew. We only recently received copies of their writings. They did say that the officers and enlisted men did not usually hang out together. Both men expressed the utmost

gratitude and respect for Brodie. Dan Kinney stated in his Memories, "Right here I'll add that the one reason I AM Alive is due to the guts and skill of our then co-pilot, Lt. Robert Brodersen (Brodie), who later became our commander."

Paul Albert quoted Brodie in his memories, "Each man owed his life to each of the others."

We should mention, Bob did keep in touch over the years with Mac McCall, the original pilot of the crew. Our family visited theirs in Maryland in 1965, and they came to Nebraska a few times.

If anything is to come out of this book, we would want you to remember to thank a veteran, they have given so much. We have had many tell us that everyone should read this Diary of Missions. It is only by looking at our history that we can truly understand and appreciate each other.

The phrase "All gave some, and some gave all" is so fitting. We cannot all be veterans, so remember to tell someone that you love and appreciate them. Every day counts. Making that happen should be our mission.

Sara Brodersen Cameron
Daughter of Robert J. Brodersen in honor of what would be his 100th birthday 5/27/2021.

www.ingramcontent.com/pod-product-compliance
Lightning Source LLC
Chambersburg PA
CBHW030826060726
47590CB00004B/1411